This book is printed for free distribution by

Khun Vanee Lamsam

in memory of

Praya and Khunying Chavakij Banharn

F R E E D O M
INDIVIDUAL AND SOCIAL

PHRA DEBVEDI
(Prayudh Payutto)

Buddhadhamma Foundation

Bangkok

Freedom, Individual and Social

ISBN 974-8358-59-3

© Phra Debvedi *(Prayudh Payutto)*

first published
January 12, 1987
Second impression
October 14, 1990

Published by

Buddhadhamma Foundation Publications
812/71 Soi Kwonthip 2, Prachachuen Rd.,
Dusit, Bangkok 10800, Thailand.
Tel. 585-1630, 585-6861

Author's Note

(Second impression)

This book was first printed in 1987, for free distribution, under the financial help of Dr. Charoon Bholanivas and became out of print not long after. This second impression, also for free distribution, has been made possible according to the wish of Khun Vanee Lamsam, who did not only urge the reprint but also sponsored all costs of publication. Her generosity deserves favor and gratitude.

I would like to thank Ven. Puriso, an Australian Bhikkhu, the abbot of Wat Keu-an in Ubolrajadhani, who kindly helped polish the language for this second impression and Khun Panya Vijinthanasarn for the cover design.

My thanks go also to Dr. Grant A. Olson who, sometime after the first impression, read the article on "Buddhism and Peace" and made valuable suggestions for language improvement, many of which I have followed.

Special thanks are due to Phramaha Insorn Duangkid for preparing the whole manuscript by the Desktop Publishing Process ready for printing, saving time, energy and funds, to Khun Chutima Thanapura who helped with proof-reading, and to Khun Panita Angchandrpen who, as with the first impression, has seen the book through all its stages.

April 1990   *Phra Debvedi (Prayudh Payutto)*

Contents

BUDDHISM AND PEACE

Logo of the International Year of Peace

Buddhism and Peace[*]

The current year of 1986 has been specially designated as the *International Year of Peace.* But when we look at the state of affairs in the world of today, we may wonder if the present time is entitled to that cheerful and honourable appellation. I think we should rather call it *The International Year in Need of Peace.* Obviously, we are now living in a period of time when the world is badly in need of peace. It is not peace that prevails in the world at this time, but its antithesis, war and violence, that is prevalent.

---

[*] A lecture delivered on December 3, 2529/1986 at the International Conference on Higher Education and the Promotion of Peace held at the Asia Hotel, Bangkok.

The International Year in Need of Peace

Instead of peace, wars and conflicts have become widespread and develop, both in kinds and in degree of fatality. People are too familiar with news and reports on racial conflicts, terrorism, ideological persecution and warfare and the proliferation of nuclear weapons, to the point of risking a nuclear war and the mass destruction of mankind. In addition to these lethal operations, so many conditions pointing to a state of social disorder and degeneration predominate, such as domestic crimes, drug addiction, environmental pollution, the energy crisis, unemployment, mental disorders, suicide and all forms of violence. Seemingly, people are turning all their efforts into making the earth an unsafe place to live. Peace and happiness seem to be farther and farther away, if not beyond reach. The various kinds of problems affecting peace are on the increase, eroding any hope of happy and peaceful living.

The official symbol or logo of the International Year of Peace is portrayed by a dove above two hands, enclosed by an olive branch. To stray a little from the traditional symbolism, the dove represents peace and the olive branch prosperity, while the two hands stand for the whole of mankind. The dove looks like it is flying out of the enclosure of the olive branch, away from the two hands, which are trying to hold it back. In an arbitrary interpretation to suit the current situation, peace has slipped out of the hands of mankind who, even though in the midst of wealth and affluence, has lost it and is desperately struggling to get it back.

It has been a hope and a dream of mankind that, with scientific and technological advances, he will be in possession of all that he wants and in control of everything he comes into contact with, and so live happily in peace. Truly, man has succeeded to a considerable extent in scientific and technological endeavours. Through scientific and technological progress, man seems to have been equipped with all that he needs to make himself and his society happy and peaceful.

However, on the contrary, problems have so increased that man himself cannot find peace and society is in turmoil. While, through medical advances, the life span of human beings has been lengthened, more and more people, including the youth, find their lives and society so unsatisfactory that they seek to shorten their lives by suicide. These people turn their hate and dissatisfaction inside to kill themselves, while many others turn it outwardly to cause conflicts with their neighbours and troubles in society. Moreover, in man's efforts to conquer nature, the natural environment has become polluted and causes many to live shorter, unhealthier lives. Nature is not on good terms with humanity. Finding no peace with nature, man's hope for happiness is even more frustrated.

All in all, man fails to realize peace and happiness; his dream does not come true. The year of peace turns out not to be the year in which peace prevails, but the year in which peace is badly needed. The road to peace turns out to be the road out of peace, and the path to happiness transforms into the path away from happiness. At least, peace and happiness are on the wane, while troubles and miseries gain eminence.

The Origins of Man's Problems

Here, the question is very simple: Why has it been so? And to this, the answer is also simple: Because the individual man has not been developed. Truly, man has greatly developed all kinds of things in the name of civilization, including science and technology, but he has paid too little attention to the development of himself. Man thinks of himself as the enjoyer of developments, not as an object of development. Human problems are, therefore, the same now as before, this year as three or ten thousand years ago, and human motives for action are of the same nature, even though they may take different forms, and the place of emphasis may change under different circumstances.

Legends and history tell us of kings, princes and warriors of yore who waged wars with one another to win the hands of beautiful princesses. Others invaded their neighbours and pillaged the towns and cities of the defeated. Today, conflicts grow between industrial powers, and we witness the trade warriors battling for resources and markets. Kings of olden times marched their troops into wars of conquest, expanding their empires in order to be hailed the greatest emperors or the most powerful conquerors. The nuclear powers of today, driven by fear of each other and the urge for primacy, engage in the arms race for military supremacy. In ancient times, fanatical rulers persecuted people of other faiths and went into religious or holy wars. Modern nations sponsor wars, both cold and active, in different parts of the world, in order to spread their political and economic "isms", or as part of their ideological propagation. Primitive peoples fought with one another, using sticks and stones. Feudal warriors fought with swords and bows. Modern soldiers also fight, but they resort to grenades and missiles for their weapons.

With the modern means of rapid and far-reaching communication and with the most efficient and powerful equipment and weapons provided by scientific and technological advances, modern problems appear in a vast variety of manifestations, affecting mankind on a wider scale and in greater severity.

In spite of all the ostensible differences, the motives behind the actions are the same ones. All forms of war, conflict, rivalry and quarrel, whether between individuals, groups or nations at the global level, whether current or in the distant past, can be traced to the same three categories of self-centred motives or tendencies, viz.,

1. Selfish desire for pleasures and acquisitions *(Taṇhā)*;
2. Egotistical lust for dominance and power *(Māna)*;
3. Clinging to view, faith or ideology *(Diṭṭhi)*.

If not refined, wisely channelled or replaced by wholesome mental qualities, these three self-centred tendencies of the mind develop and intensify, so that the behaviour of the person becomes dangerous to others and to society.

First, *the selfish desire for pleasures and acquisitions* leads to attachment to wealth and greed for possessions. Its influence in causing crime, exploitation, corruption and conflict is too obvious, needing no description. This also explains why, while the wealth-creating possibilities of new technology now seem boundless, the gap between the rich and the poor widens, the polarization of wealth and poverty becoming stronger and sharper.

New agricultural technologies have made 'food for all' a perfectly realizable objective, yet starvation is widespread and hundreds of thousands of human beings starve to death. The advanced technology and new economic approaches are utilized in such a way that they serve the industrialized countries only for making more profit, and developing countries only help to strengthen the economies of the developed ones. The profit-maximizing approach of the current economic system and the consumer culture serve only to divert world savings away from developing countries and make richer the developed countries. Modern modes of production lead to the benefits of capital accumulation. While costs are borne by all, benefits accrue to a few; the rich become richer and the poor poorer. The number of what the World Bank calls the "absolute poor" is around 800 million. In spite of many foreign aid programmes and advances in production technology, the world faces an economic crisis. The unequal distribution of wealth still prevails. Moreover, craving for sensual enjoyment and sensual indulgence lead to the lavish consumption of natural resources and the polluting of the environment, resulting in the depletion of resources, health problems and the aggravation of poverty. With hunger and mass misery prevailing, the risk of war increases and world peace is unrealizable.

Secondly, with *craving for dominance and lust for power,* individuals, parties and nations vie with one another for primacy or superiority. With hostile attitudes, some come into quarrels, conflict and wars. Even in the absence of an open conflict, they live in fear, distrust and anxiety. At national and international levels, this is detrimental to mutual security and development. Political leaders resort to arms as props for political power. Developed countries lend aid to developing countries with ulterior motives, for their own benefit, including the creation of a permanent dependance. At the same time, many people in developing countries are careless and dishonest in the handling of aid and loans. Foreign aid programmes are surrounded by a climate of disillusion and distrust.

At the global level, the world has for many decades been dominated by the hostile relationships of the superpowers, in their quest for security and superiority through the arms race. World military expenditure is well over $1.5 million every minute of every day. A UNDP administrator in his statement to the UN General Assembly Second Special Disarmament Session in 1982 said:

"All the technical cooperation UNDP has been charged to provide to developing countries over the next five years will cost less than the sum that will be consumed in world armaments expenditures in the next four days."[1]

The late Lord Philip Noel-Baker, at a conference in London in January 1977, said to the effect that for an expenditure of $500 million, about the cost of an aircraft carrier, the WHO could eliminate malaria, trachoma, leprosy and yaws—the four diseases that impose a heavy load of economic loss and human suffering on the Third World—forever.[2]

This shows how human, material and financial resources have been used far more for negative and destructive purposes than for positive and constructive purposes. It is evident how the arms

---

[1-2] Quoted in Inga Thorsson, "Disarmament and Development," *Third World Affairs 1986* (London: The Eastern Press Ltd. for Third World Foundation for Social and Economic Studies, 1986), p.368

race is worsening the economic crisis and making the world over-armed and undernourished. The arms race is a threat to world security and human survival, both militarily and economically. Militarily, the military forces and arsenals of the superpowers have grown far beyond their defensive requirements, to the capability of eradicating all life from the earth, a threat to all mankind. Economically, as the arms race and development compete for the same resources, the immensely rising world-wide military expenditures have strong negative effects on economic growth and development and human welfare in general. The nuclear arsenals kill millions of human beings even without being used, because they eat up the resources without which people are put to death by starvation. With or without wars, human society cannot fare happily in peace.

Thirdly, last in order but not least in controlling power, is *clinging to view, theory, faith or ideology.* Since ancient times, owing to differences in faith and beliefs, people have come into conflict. Some waged wars with their neighbours out of religious fanaticism, some even marching their armies to faraway lands, to force their faiths on other peoples and make conquests in the name of their Supreme Being. While conflicts between religious groups and factions still continue today, modern people add the wars and conflicts of economic systems and political ideologies. Nations even divide into competing ideological blocs. Religious and ideological persecutions and wars, both cold and active, between religious groups and factions, and between those who quarrel about different ideas for the best way to achieve happiness for all, can be found in many parts of the world, dominating all other kinds of conflicts. Predictably, not finding any peaceful means of ideological propagation and coexistence, what will prevail is not the world peace and happiness that those faiths and ideologies prescribe, but human suffering and death.

On the present-day global scene of conflicts and wars, it is not specifically any one of these three motives that drives peoples to the battlefield, but rather all three of them combined together that come into play; and their combination only makes the situation more serious, the problem more complicated and the solution more difficult to achieve.

For example, behind the fighting between two religious or ideological groups in a small country, two big powers vying with each other for the domination of this country may be backing the two warring parties, one on each side, by providing them with supplies of weapons, and simultaneously making profit through arms sales, or keeping the smaller countries in a state of dependency through indebtedness. Employers want to pay the least and get the most profit, while employees want to work the least and be paid the highest wages. While each party desires to take advantage of the other, the two come into conflict. Competing to win, they try to gain dominance over each other. To strengthen their own confidence and their claims and complaints, they turn for support to economic ideologies. A conflict of gains becomes also a conflict of ideologies. In an ideological conflict, ideological sympathizers and partisans take sides. The conflict then grows in all possible ways, at the expense of the hope for peace.

The Undeveloped Condition of Man

How can we stop wars and conflicts? How can we be sure that peace will prevail and become long-lasting? Some might say that love and cooperation must be established in place of competition and conflict. This seems to be too easy an answer. It looks impractical. We have to further ask: How can we turn hostility and conflict into love and cooperation? So long as man is overcome by any of the three self-centred tendencies, true love and cooperation are impossible. If he acts out of any of them, he cannot be on good terms with others. He will only hurt them and cause in them hatred and anger. With his own desire countered, challenged or defied, he himself develops anger and hatred. From anger and hatred ensue only hostility and conflict, not love, cooperation or peace.

For people who are in conflict, one or the other must first act for peace. But for them, such action would mean a loss. They would say that they are forced to struggle to win, that there is no other choice. The real solution must be made before the conflict starts. To put it more correctly, there must be a fundamental change in the behaviour of man, in such a way that he will no more engage in conflict. To get to a real, practical solution, we must turn to the answer to a more fundamental question.

Enabled by science and technology to increase both the capability to solve most problems and the capacity to destroy everything, why does man tend to choose the latter? Why has the abundance of human talent and material resources been devoted to such negative and destructive purposes as arms buildups and militarization, instead of being positively utilized in developing the means for securing a stable and lasting peace? As given earlier, the answer is simple: Because man has been so engrossed in the development of things outside that he has neglected the task of developing himself, leaving himself almost an unchanged being, who follows the driving forces of instinct, rather than the guidance of wisdom. Professor Albert Einstein accepted this when he said that the atomic bomb had changed everything except the mind and the thinking of people.[3]

Science and technology serve to advance the frontiers of human knowledge and potential, either for better or for worse. They provide man with free and full scope to exercise his free will on the material world. If he acts in the direction of peace and happiness, everything on earth is on his side to achieve it. If his action turns towards war and misery, he can exterminate the whole race of mankind in a matter of seconds. Which direction he will take is the question of human development. If man has developed himself properly, he will be able to steer technology and all other vehicles of civilization towards the goal of peace and mutual well-being.

---

[3] Quoted in Willy Brandt, "Peace and Development (Third World Lecture 1985)," *Third World Affairs 1986,* P.350

Unfortunately, the development of the inner core of man, the mind, the formation of character and spiritual values, has not kept pace with the rapid progress of technology. Though he has developed technical capabilities to the highest possible degree, man still has not developed in himself the qualities needed to live and to deal with his own self, with others and with his natural and technological environment.

The undeveloped or underdeveloped condition of man, of his mind and character, and of his liberating wisdom, is discernible in many ways:

First, man behaves wrongly and unwisely in relation to happiness. Man looks at happiness as something he is in search of, that is, something unattained, not already in hand. In other words, man himself is here and now not happy and he is looking for something to make himself happy. With this attitude, he mistreats happiness both in time and in space. In time, happiness is for him a state he hopes to realize some time in the future, something in prospect. In space, happiness is for him a state to be attained to by satisfying himself with something found or obtained from outside, an external object. Either way, he cannot find true happiness. The unhappy man has to run forever after happiness, and also has to depend for happiness on things outside of his control. Many people would even sacrifice their already existing happiness, essentially the inner peace and happiness of the mind, to chase the hoped-for happiness, like the dog that drops the piece of meat in its mouth in the hope of catching the other piece seen reflected in a pond. If he succeeds, he gets a superficial happiness, at the cost of the profound one. If he does not, his loss is twofold and anguish is his lot.

In the contest of running to grab pleasure-giving objects, the unhappy people unavoidably come into conflict. Moreover, their restless search for happiness goes on at the expense of inner happiness and peace of mind. Thus, in this process of ever running after pleasure, peace and happiness are not to be found either within or without. This also shows how unscientific people are. Modern people may have scientific attitudes towards the whole universe, but that covers only the material world of phenomena. Regarding themselves, their life and mind, their approaches are not scientific at all. The way they treat their lives and deal with peace and happiness is scientifically irrational.

In the right and proper way, man must be made happy here and now, not relying on hoped-for pleasures from outside. For the happy person, pleasures that are upcoming only enhance happiness. But, for the unhappy, or the happy-to-be person, these coming pleasures can only give extraneous and ephemeral satisfaction, bringing anxiety and tension with their coming and leaving regret and sorrow in their wake. Just as the beauty wrought by cosmetics and decoration is not the real beauty, even so the happiness of external pleasure is not the real happiness. And just as cosmetics and decoration can enhance real beauty, even so extraneous pleasures can enhance real happiness. Emphatically, it is not merely a matter of real or unreal happiness, but that of the lack of real happiness which leads to trouble and conflict in society. Therefore, first and before all else, the making of a happy person is the prerequisite for peace, and the development of the individual is the central question of development.

Secondly, the unhappy person, in his efforts to find something to make himself happy, causes even more trouble by resorting to wrong means for obtaining it. He seeks enjoyment at the expense of others. As a man who seeks pleasure by going fishing with rod and line enjoys himself by causing suffering to the fish, people tend to seek happiness by, either directly or indirectly, hurting others. At least, they do not care what will happen to other lives or the world of nature as a result of their selfish acts. From this spring conflicts and many other problems, such as violations of human rights, injustice, poverty and environmental pollution.

In such an unfriendly and depressed atmosphere, they themselves cannot enjoy real peace and happiness. As the Buddha said: Whoever seeks happiness by inflicting suffering on others is enmeshed in hostile relations and will not be free from enmity.[4] In fact, it is the one who hurts who will first be hurt, rather than those he wants to cause loss and trouble to. In the words of the Buddha: A man spoils himself first before he hurts others.[5] Some people even seek to enjoy themselves at the expense of their own lives. Drug addicts and alcoholics are among this kind of people. All the pleasure seeking activities of these unhappy people are inhibitions to peaceful living. They form the behavioural pattern of an undeveloped or underdeveloped person.

A developed person is, on the contrary, happy of his own nature as a result of self-development, and seeks to enjoy himself by means of what brings happiness both to himself and to others. In other words, a developed person is characterized by his inherent happiness and his way of enjoying himself,

---

[4] Dh.291 (Dhammapada, verse no.291)
[5] A.III.373 (Anguttara-Nikāya, vol.III, p.373)

in which he diffuses happiness among people throughout society.

To put it another way, a person in his relationship with other people, both consciously and unconsciously, shares with the latter what he has. If he has happiness, he gives out happiness. If he has unhappiness, he gives out unhappiness. The unhappy person, in particular, is weighed down with his unhappiness and, in an effort to get rid of it, he desperately throws it off onto the people around him. Thus, the undeveloped, unhappy person will render a peaceful society an impossibility. Therefore, it is imperative that people be developed to be happy if any hope for peace is to be realized.

Again, so many people in this technological age, having succeeded in obtaining material gains and sensual pleasures to gratify their desires, in no long time find that they become bored and discontented, feeling that these gains and pleasures do not give them real happiness. Tired of the ceaseless, unsuccessful quest for happiness, surrounded by the ever-increasing, unsolved problems rampant in society and all over the world, and finding no better means of realizing happiness, these people become bored, frustrated, anxious and confused. They live unhappily, without peace of mind. This condition is growing to be characteristic of present-day society.

In sum, the failure of man to secure peace and happiness lies in that, being unhappy and not training himself to be happy, man struggles in vain to realize peace and happiness by setting out in these two wrong ways. He seeks to make himself happy with pleasures from outside, and in so doing covers up, or plasters over, his unhappiness with extraneous pleasures. As the person himself has not been changed, the process of covering or plastering has to run on endlessly. And as it is there deep inside, the unhappiness will never vanish, despite any amount of plaster or cover up. Simultaneously, as this process of unrestrained pursuit of ever-increasing pleasures has to go on at the expense of, or in competition with, other people, it results in hate, anger, trouble, conflict and the loss of peace and happiness, both in the mind of the individual and in society. Alternatively, the person, with his inherent unhappiness, seeks to make himself happy by giving out or throwing off his unhappiness onto others. Other people then react and retaliate in kind, and possibly in a higher degree of severity. In this way also, instead of finding real happiness, he only increases, intensifies and spreads unhappiness far and wide.

Thus, the process of the human search for happiness becomes the process of driving peace away. In other words, desiring one thing, man creates the cause for the arising of another. Desiring happiness, he creates the cause for suffering. Desiring peace, he creates the cause for hatred and conflict.

Freedom As the Guaranty of Peace and Happiness

In Buddhism, peace *(Santi)* and happiness *(Sukha)* are synonymous. An unhappy person cannot find peace, and there can be no peace without happiness. In the absence of peace, no people can be happy, and those who are unhappy cannot live in peace. The Buddha said: There is no happiness beyond peace.[6] However, it is of much significance to note that Buddhism prescribes freedom as another synonym for peace and happiness. Only the free person can be possessed of peace and happiness. Endowed with freedom, people can live happy and peaceful lives. There are roughly *four levels of freedom,* the achievement of which is indispensable for the realization of peace and happiness, viz.,

1. Physical freedom, or freedom in relation to the material world or physical environment, natural or technological. This covers freedom from the

---

[6] Dh.202 (Dhammapada, verse no.202)

shortage of the basic needs of life, the requisites of food, clothing, shelter and health-care; freedom consisting in safety from life-threatening calamities and unfavourable natural conditions, i.e. to have, among other things, a beneficial natural environment; the wise use of natural resources, the requisites of life and technology in such a way that they serve man to enhance his quality of life and do not subject him to themselves for his good or evil, happiness or sorrow.

2. *Social freedom,* or freedom in relation to other people, the community, society or social environment. This is represented by freedom from oppression, persecution, exploitation, injustice, crimes, the violation of human rights, discrimination, violence, terrorism, conflict, fighting and war; the non-violation of the Five Precepts; or, in positive terms, a good and friendly relationship with neighbours, social welfare and such values as equality, liberty, fraternity, discipline, respect for law, tolerance and cooperation.

3. Emotional freedom, or freedom of the heart. At the ideal level, this refers to the state of freedom from all traces of mental defilements and suffering, the state of mind that is unshaken by worldly vicissitudes, purified, sorrow-free, secure, and profoundly happy and peaceful, i.e. *Nibbāna.* It includes freedom from all kinds of mental illness, stress and strain, anxiety, boredom, fear, depression, greed, jealousy, hatred, ill will, sloth, restlessness, remorse and uncertainty; or, in positive terms, the state of being endowed with such beneficial mental qualities as love, compassion, sympathetic joy, equanimity, confidence, mindfulness, conscience, forbearance, generosity, tranquillity, concentration, mental strength and firmness and perfect mental health, consisting of mental clarity and purity, peacefulness and happiness.

4. Intellectual freedom, or freedom of and through knowledge and wisdom. Belonging to this class of freedom are: the process of perceiving and learning that is clear of and free from distortion by any bias or ulterior motives; freedom of thinking and judgement and the free exercise of knowledge and wisdom that are just, honest, sincere and accurate, not influenced by prejudices, self-interest, greed, hatred or any selfish motives; and the knowledge of all things as they really are, or the insight into the true nature of all things, together with the emotional freedom as its corollary and the life-view and world-view that are based on that knowledge.

These four levels of freedom can be reclassified as three by putting the third and the fourth levels together as one and the same level of spiritual or individual freedom.

The four (or three) levels of freedom are interrelated and interdependent. Without a minimum of physical freedom, the road to the other three levels of freedom is blocked. Without intellectual and emotional freedom, the wise use of resources as physical freedom is rendered impossible. Lacking the freedom of knowledge and wisdom, the mind cannot be set free. In the absence of the freedom of the heart, social freedom is only a dream. Except for social freedom, physical freedom cannot come true.

With this fourfold freedom, peace and happiness are surely secured and they are real peace and real happiness, found both within and without, that is, peace and happiness that are deep-rooted in the mind of the individual and prevalent outside in society.

Under physical freedom, man is relatively free from the oppression of nature and he also does not exploit or spoil nature, but makes wise and unselfish use of natural resources to achieve mutual well-being both of man and of nature. He thus lives in peace with nature. Equipped with all kinds of facilities provided by science and technology as his servant, not himself turning into their slave, man can be said to have fulfilled the physical aspect of the good or ideal life. With this physical freedom as a firm foundation, man is in a good position to realize the other three aspects of freedom.

Proper Assessment of Science and Technology

With such obvious advances in science and technology, man should have achieved physical freedom. However, on the contrary, it turns out that despite all the scientific and technological achievements, the problems of human suffering, even at the physical level, instead of decreasing, are on the increase. This seems to be the dilemma of human progress. The answer lies partly in the disenchantment of man with the wish-granting power of science and technology and partly in the readjustment of man's relationship with the same.

So far, man seems to have put too much trust in science and technology, as if they were the sole designer of his ideal life, and to have increasingly been dependent on them to the ignorance and neglect of the development of himself. He does not realize that the fulfilment of a good life depends on himself, the one who created and who is served by science and technology. He himself needs to be so developed that he can master the service and control of science and technology for his own freedom and well-being. Otherwise, he himself may be dominated or exterminated by what he has created. Then, science and technology would be like a monster, created by man to do everything for him, but which later, being of greater power and capability than man, turned to dominate him and, in the end, put him to death.

Man has been so much enchanted by scientific and technological progress that he has become misled into believing that he has almost completely conquered nature and has control over it. He also believes that with this conquest of nature, all problems will be solved and heaven will be established on earth. But he is not aware that the nature that he thinks he has conquered is not the whole picture, but only a part of it, possibly a half of it, that is, the external material world. The other half is within himself, the nature of man or man as a part of nature. In the process of struggling to conquer the material world of nature, man often neglects his responsibility to master the inner nature within himself and tends to lose control over it. Conversely, this inner nature has grown stronger and stronger and has largely taken control over man. In other words, though Prometheus was unbound a long time ago, until now he has not found freedom. He has gone astray and there is a fear that he is about to be bound again, this time by a monster-like robot.

Thus, in looking outside with a pride that he has conquered nature, man has unconsciously been conquered by the nature inside himself and obediently come under its control. It is this unconquered controlling nature within man that has frustrated all his hopes of turning the earth into paradise. It is this nature that keeps the inner man unhappy under the plaster of a happiness-like pleasure, and causes the unhappy man to diffuse unhappiness, and the unpeaceful man to diffuse peacelessness, violence and conflict in society. This also explains why so many efficient and effective methods and measures to solve the various problems of mankind do not work out.

By way of illustration, when the abundance of consumer goods more than adequate to satisfy the basic needs of people has been made possible by scientific and technological advances, and only proper distribution is needed to achieve mutual well-being, it is often not distribution that is carried out but appropriation resulting in poverty and conflict instead of peace and well-being. This is also true with the different groups, factions, parties and nations who cannot clear up their differences, who start armed conflicts, and continue to fight, not-withstanding the solution seeming very simple and easy.

Modern people are proud that they have a scientific attitude towards things. However, it is a pity that their attitude to science and technology is less scientific than it should be. They do not know science and technology as they really are and thus cannot deal with them in a scientific way. This also implies that their knowledge of nature is still inadequate, so that they cannot maintain a right and proper relationship with it.

In answering the question of how man can realize freedom, we should have a knowledge of the true nature of science and technology, their extent and limitations, their capabilities and incapabilities. Scientific knowledge is limited to the data received through the sense organs. Its domain is the material world, its knowledge of which is really enormous. However, science knows only little about the individual man. When people are depressed and frustrated and their minds are filled with fear, unrest and anxiety, science and technology can be of no sound and substantial help. Crimes, violence and various kinds of immoral acts still abound, even in the countries which are most advanced in science and technology. Science and technology are unable to make man better. Despite all the advances in science and technology, the inner person is left basically unchanged. Modern problems remain the same in nature as those afflicting our ancestors.

They differ only in the matter of their greater number, wider variety and greater magnitude.

With the unprecedented availability of all kinds of advantages, science and technology bring to the undeveloped person only heightened feelings of dependence and insufficiency, and, with their destructive potential, they make one feel even more insecure. Science and technology have rendered great help to mankind in the conquest of nature—here, the material world—but they cannot give him moral guidance and control over his mind. He may be able to conquer the world but cannot conquer himself. The individual, the mind, his inner nature and his development, along with his real peace and happiness, are beyond the domain of science and technology. They are not their province but the domain of the Dhamma, or religion in a special sense of the term.

Accordingly, we have here two complementary domains of human quest for freedom and perfection, the inner and the outer ones. Preoccupation with the outer domain to the ignorance or neglect of the inner one leads only to partial success or even to total failure. Success in achieving freedom, peace and happiness for man lies in the proper recognition and understanding of the nature, significance, capacity and limitations of each of these two domains as they really are, and in the attitudes and practices in conformity with such understanding.

The Loss of the Way to Freedom

The process by which to achieve freedom (and peace and happiness) is called development *(bhāvanā)*, and in Buddhism, as far as man is concerned, development is synonymous with education *(sikkhā)*. Just as freedom is of four levels, development or education is fourfold, viz., *physical development*, leading to physical freedom, *social development*, leading to social freedom, *emotional development*, leading to emotional freedom, and *intellectual development,* leading to intellectual freedom.

As for physical freedom and physical development, a considerable contribution to success must be credited to science and technology. The immense achievements of science and technology must be appreciated. They must not be underestimated, though also not exaggerated. Through scientific and technological development, great material abundance has been provided, to such an extent that goods and facilities are more than enough to serve all people to make them happy. Science and technology have brought physical freedom within easy reach. It is up to people themselves whether they will utilize them to contribute to their happiness or to their unhappiness. In other words, people of today are equipped with almost unbounded technological potential, either for positive purposes, to make all people live in affluence, or for negative purposes, to put mankind to wholesale destruction. Here end the function and responsibility of science and technology.

Nature may be increasingly produced by certain groups in the interests of wealth accumulation, thereby widening the gap between the rich and the poor and causing prevalent poverty and starvation; greater and greater amounts of money may be spent on the arms race to serve the international power contest, indirectly rendering food, education and health care inaccessible to large numbers of people through misdirection of resources; more and more people may die in armed conflicts between religious groups and ideological parties who resort to force and might for the decision of who is right and who is wrong, or what is true and what is false; natural resources may be selfishly exploited and lavishly consumed in such manner as to cause resource depletion and environmental pollution. If such problems arise, it is not science and technology that are to blame. The fault lies with mankind himself, who fails to make wise and proper use of science and technology, but seeks their services as occasions for the discharge and maximization of his three self-centred tendencies, or impulses, of selfish desire for pleasures and acquisitions, egotistical lust for dominance and power, and clinging to views and ideologies. How can we find fault with them while scientific and technological developments are merely products of human creation?

The One Solution

Now, it is at this point that the contribution or complementary service of true religion, or the Dhamma, is needed. It is needed for the development of the individual himself, so that he will create only constructive technology and make wise and proper use of science, technology and resources, both human and natural, for beneficial purposes, to realize a good life and society for all mankind.

Right education or the *right development of man* is the long-term and sole solution to the problems of man. It entails a fundamental change in the pattern of human thinking and behaviour. Any proposed solutions other than this are superficial and impractical. We may propose many shortcut methods which make the solution seemingly easy, but there will be too many *ifs* which cannot be removed and lead only to an impasse. Words may sound very beautiful, but they are lacking in practicability.

For example, in a conflict or an arms race, we may say that if one party stops, problems will be solved. But, in practice, the rivals will dispute as to who will be the first to stop. Naturally unable to agree, they each would complain that they are forced to take action or to struggle for primacy, there being no other choice. As a result, the conflict or the arms race continues and becomes increasingly intensified. This is the usual pattern of thought and behaviour of the undeveloped man, which leads to problems and needs to be changed if any solution is to be realized.

The undeveloped man thinks arbitrarily, unsystematically, at random, usually under the influence of passing motives or inherent tendencies. When science and technology come, he is taught and trained to think systematically. He then thinks in terms of science and technology. In terms of science, he thinks: What is it? along with all the facts and data such as hows and whys about that thing or phenomenon. This may be followed by a thought in terms of technology: What is the use of it? What use can we make of it? or: How can it be turned into use? Here ends the thought in terms of science and technology. Beyond this point, man again thinks at random or habitually, influenced by selfish motives or inherent tendencies.

Thus, scientific and technological thinking does not make any fundamental change in man's pattern of thought and behaviour, it makes no development of the thinking man. Moreover, it leaves a wide gap in the thinking process of man, the gap in which his habitual thinking, under the influence of inbred motives and tendencies, will follow and exploit scientific and technological thinking. Thus, scientific and technological thought is at the service of habitual and arbitrary thinking and serves to expand the dimension and magnitude of the latter. The motives or tendencies to be served are usually the three self-centred ones mentioned above.

Following the first phase of scientific thinking, "What, how and why is it?" and the second phase of technological thinking, "What is the use of it? How can it be put into use?" man further thinks: "How can I make use of it to gain profit or for my enjoyment? How can I use it to dominate my neighbours, to show my eminence over them, to put them in my service? How can I use it to win people over to my opinion, to my faith? How can I use it to press them to accept my theory or ideology?" The thinking process of man can thus be shown in three phases, in terms of science, of technology and of exploitation. Certainly, it is the third phase of thinking that will direct and control the ensuing behaviour and actions. Then, beginning with selfishness both within the mind itself and pervading the whole process, the hope for peace is surely to be frustrated.

Development of Man As the Prerequisite for Peace

It is at this point that we need amendment, and the service of religion, or the Dhamma, is indispensable. This means that systematic thinking, free of harmful motives and self-centered tendencies, must continue, following the first and second phases of scientific and technological thinking, into the third decisive phase. People have to be trained to think in terms of ethical or moral values such as: How can this be used to enhance the quality of life or to promote the mutual well-being of mankind? If moral thought has been established as the third phase of the thinking process, moral behaviour and actions will follow, completing a whole process and leaving no gap for unwholesome tendencies to influence. Now the thinking process consists of the three phases of thinking in terms of science, of technology, and of ethical values. Thus, science, technology and the Dhamma or religion are harmoniously integrated even at the level of thought, each finding its proper role which is complementary to the others. A fundamental change in the pattern of thought and behaviour has also been achieved.

However, it is not necessary that the thinking process will consist of all these three phases. The scientific and technological phases exemplify neutral phases in general. They can be dropped or replaced by some or other neutral phases. Only the Dhamma or ethical phase is a necessity. Both moral and immoral tendencies are there in the mind. If the moral ones are not to the fore, the immoral will come to reign. (However, with true knowledge or insight into the true nature of things, which usually requires mental training, a man can have a pure process of thought, beyond both moral and immoral qualities.)

Today, *how to think* is an emphasis in education. Truly, children, and all people alike, should be taught how to think. Many people, however, refer to the "how to think" only in terms of scientific or intellectual thinking. They do not touch the true nature of the mind and thus leave the thinking process unsound and defective. Their "how to think" is therefore too short to realize the aim of education, that is, to develop the individual man so that human problems will be rightly solved and a good life will be attained to. With the phase of moral thought, the thinking process of "how to think" is complete. In this right process of thinking, intellectual thought and moral thought become integrated. It is thought that is both rational, wholesome and truly sound. Then "how to think" means the way of thinking which is in accordance with truth, full of reason, and favourable to a good life. With this right thought, true religion is there in man. He is truly religious in the full sense of the term (religion in the meaning of the Dhamma). There is no need for any other label.

The right process of thinking as described above is the connection through which mental or emotional development can induce and occasion physical and social development, and through which mental or emotional freedom can contribute to the achievement of, or even effectuate, physical and social freedom.

Deeper into the sphere of mental or emotional development is the readjustment or purification of the contents of the mind itself. This aims at the liberation of man from the influence or controlling power of unwholesome motives, impulses and tendencies, so that none of them will remain to overcome the thinking process. This is centred on the eradication of the three above-mentioned self-centred tendencies, that is, selfish desire for pleasures and acquisitions, egotistical lust for dominance and power, and clinging to views, faiths and ideologies. In place of these three unwholesome qualities, their three opposite ethical values will be developed respectively, viz.,

1. Wise dealing with pleasures and possessions and the resolve to make use of wealth to

realize common well-being, or wealth for the common weal.

2. Respect for, and appreciation of, the value of life, the ways of other people, and social order.

3. Detached search for truth, with an attitude of tolerance and good will to those who have different views of truth.

Usually, the three self-centred tendencies are not immediately given up by generating the three counter-values, and the latter also are usually not directly brought about to replace the former. The destruction of the former and the growth of the latter are, as a rule, the corollaries of the development of such virtues as loving-kindness, compassion, sympathetic joy and equanimity, and the practice of such ethical principles as generosity, kindly speech, life of service, and equality consisting of impartiality and participation.

The development of the heart needs a great deal of contribution from the development of wisdom, as the real freedom of the heart can be realized only through the freedom of true knowledge or wisdom. Accordingly, the total eradication of the three self-centred tendencies will be actualized only when one has attained Enlightenment, or the full understanding of life. When wisdom is lacking, or still in the early stages of its development, man has to depend on the three self-centred tendencies for his self-protection, though he has to risk their harmful influence. Once wisdom or true knowledge has been developed to the full, a person, living under the guidance of wisdom, can do away with all of them.

The term intellectual development is here loosely used. It does not exactly convey the intended meaning. It is truly not only the development of the intellect, but the development of wisdom or true knowledge.

There are so many practices that are helpful to the development of the heart. Some bring about temporary freedom. Others lead to absolute freedom.

What distinguishes them is wisdom, true knowledge or insight. Any practice without wisdom as a factor can help achieve only temporary freedom. This is evident in the practice of meditation. Generally speaking, there are two kinds of meditation: *calming meditation* and *insight meditation.* Calming meditation with concentration as its essence leads to temporary freedom. Insight meditation, in which knowledge of the true nature of things is the guiding principle, makes possible the absolute freedom. Wherever there is freedom, there are peace and happiness. Along with temporary freedom, come temporary peace and happiness. Inseparable from absolute freedom are perfect peace and happiness.

The really happy person is in real possession of happiness, as it is inside oneself. If one is provided with pleasures, one enjoys happiness to the full. If one is deprived of pleasures, or if some misfortunes befall one, one can still find happiness. The plaster of unhappiness does not have any real effect on one. Only the really happy person has real peace. Only the person who has peace can be really happy. The person who has happiness radiates happiness. The person who has peace diffuses peace. The person who has no peace of mind tends to break peace in one's family, among neighbours and wherever one is. The one who is at peace with oneself naturally and automatically lives in peace with everyone. This is the happy and peaceful person in the full sense of the terms. One's peace and happiness are true to life; and it is this truly happy and peaceful person who is the fully developed human being. One is really educated. The development that creates this free, peaceful and happy person is entitled to the term Peace Education.

In order to achieve freedom, peace and happiness for man and his society, we need the interrelated and interdependent service of the four spheres of development, and also the interrelated and interdependent fulfilment of the four levels of freedom. In the process of successful development we have to deal wisely with the two principal domains that affect man's life, i.e. the inner world of the individual himself and the outer physical world. Success in the solution of problems, and the creation of peace, lies in the right understanding and proper recognition of the relationship between the two domains, and of the extent and limitations of the roles and contributing capabilities of each of them, and in action in accordance therewith.

Regarding the outer world, we have to appreciate the roles of science and technology and the various social institutions in the process of development that leads to freedom. We must accept that science and technology rightly and wisely used can be complementary to the Dhamma, or religion, in carrying out physical development to achieve physical freedom. Effective and efficient social, economic and political systems and organizations are indispensable if social development is ever to effectuate social freedom.

However, it seems that today we already have so abundant a supply of these physical and social tools of development that there is a problem of misusing them and people, being unprepared for the wise and right use of them, gain more troubles rather than benefit from them. Now, we should stop giving them priority. Although some among us should go on with the job of improving and advancing science, technology and social, economic and political systems, special attention should be paid to the comparatively long neglected task of developing the human individual. The development of man should be our top priority of today.

The development or education of man is a unique task. It is the task of and for the specific life of each person. Unlike other fields of human activities, where the wealth of experiences and achievements of former generations can be handed down as cultural heritage to a later generation, and the later generation can make use of that heap of accumulations as the step on which they climb further up the ladder of civilization, without the necessity of starting up anew from the ground, the development or education of man is a matter for a specific life. It has to be started anew from the ground up to the top of the ladder in the span of each and every life. In considering the fact that man is the creator, the central figure and the sufferer or enjoyer of all problems and their solutions, this task is of even greater importance.

The peace and happiness of the individual are the foundation of the peace and happiness of the whole world. Education for the promotion of peace is therefore one of the most important tasks to undertake. Essentially it is education or the development of man that is the prerequisite for peace. If this right education has been fully and thoroughly carried out, the international year in need of peace will surely become the real **International Year of Peace,** when *peace, happiness* and *freedom* prevail all over the world. Or, as this year of 1986 is going to end soon, let us hope that it will be the year when the world begins to move in the right direction towards peace. Also, let everyone of us take some action to turn hope into reality.

To be practical, the first action to take is to make our own mind happy and peaceful, and then share our peace and happiness with all other people we come into contact with. May all be happy and peaceful and their mental, verbal and physical actions be contributions to the creation of long years of peace to come.

Peace be unto you and to all beings.

SANGHA:
THE IDEAL WORLD COMMUNITY

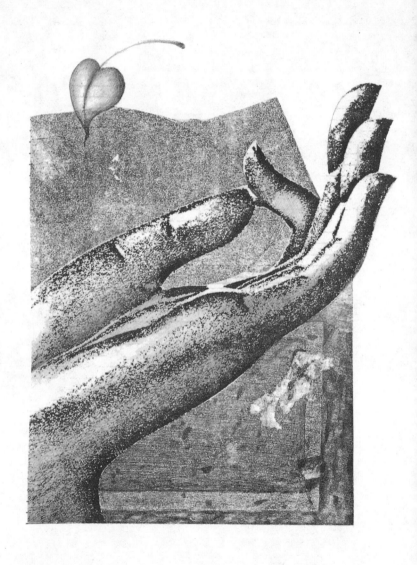

Sangha:

The Ideal World Community*

As we all know well, two months after the Enlightenment, on the full moon of the eighth lunar month, the Buddha preached his First Sermon at the Deer Park in Isipatana. The First Sermon is called the *Dhammacakkappavattana-Sutta* or the Setting in Motion of the Wheel of the Dhamma. On hearing this, *Koṇḍañña,* one of the five ascetics who had waited upon the Bodhisatta when he was practising self-mortification, gained the Eye of Truth (Dhamma-cakkhu), or the Wisdom Eye, as a first glimpse of *Nibbāna. Koṇḍañña* asked the Buddha for ordination and was admitted as a Bhikkhu, becoming

---

* A lecture delivered on January 9, 2529/1986 at the 4th International Congress of the World Buddhist Sangha Council, held at Buddha's Light Vihara, Bangkok.

the first member of the Sangha, or the Buddhist Order of monks. He is thus generally known as the Buddha's *First Disciple*. As until that time there had appeared in the world only the Buddha and the Dhamma, this event marks the completion of the Triple Gem of the Buddha, the Dhamma and the Sangha.

What should be noted here is the arising of the Sangha. Strictly speaking, it was the arising of the first member of the Sangha. That is, *Koṇḍañña,* who since then became known as *Aññākoṇḍañña,* was the first man to see the Truth after the Buddha and also the first to be admitted as a Bhikkhu.

Two Kinds of Sangha

The term Sangha means an assembly or a community. Here again, two kinds of Sangha should be distinguished, namely, the *Sāvaka-Sangha,* or the community of (noble) disciples, and the *Bhikkhu-Sangha,* or the community of Bhikkhus or monks. The former is also called the *Ariya-Sangha,* or the

Noble Sangha (community of Noble or Truly-Civilized Ones), while the latter is also named the *Sammati-Sangha,* or the conventional Sangha. The Noble Sangha of truly civilized people is formed of four types of persons, who are at four different stages of development, or levels of insight into the Truth. The Conventional Sangha of Bhikkhus, on the other hand, simply consists of four or more monks.

When *Koṇḍañña* gained the Eye of Truth, he became the first member of the Noble Sangha. When he was ordained a Bhikkhu, he became the first member of the Conventional Sangha. Thus, the event of the First Sermon marks the beginning both of the Noble Sangha of disciples and of the Conventional Sangha of monks.

The four types of persons who form the Noble Sangha are the *Sotāpanna* or Stream-Enterers (those who have entered the stream leading to Nibbāna), the *Sakadāgāmī* or Once-Returners (those who will return only once more to the vicissitudes of this world), the *Anāgāmī* or Non-Returners (those who will never come again to the dubious conditions of this world), and the *Arahants* or Worthy Ones (those who have achieved the ideal of perfection and attained to the goal of Nibbāna).

The *Sotāpanna* has achieved perfection in morality and has abandoned the three fetters of self-illusion, uncertainty and clinging to mere rules and ritual. The *Sakadāgāmī* has in addition mitigated lust, hatred and delusion. The *Anāgāmī* has achieved perfection in mental discipline and further eradicated the fetters of sensual lust and ill will. The *Arahant* has achieved perfection in wisdom and put an end to five more fetters, namely, attachment to fine-material existence, attachment to immaterial existence, conceit, restlessness and ignorance.

The Monastic Sangha and the Creation of the Noble Sangha

Obviously, it is the purpose of the Buddha, in his conduct for the well-being of the world, to teach all people to progress along these lines of development to become *Sotāpanna,* *Sakadāgāmī,* *Anāgāmī* and *Arahants.* In other words, he wants them to be members of the Noble Sangha. The ideal is surely to turn the world into a community of noble or truly civilized people. To achieve this, however, a sound concrete organization is needed, and it is for this reason that the Conventional Sangha of monks was founded. Truly, the Sangha of monks or Bhikkhu-Sangha has been vested with the main function of teaching all people, regardless of caste, class, sex and nationality, the Dhamma that will help them in their self-development to become *Ariya* or *Ārya* (noble or truly civilized). The monks thus lead the people in creating the universal community of noble, enlightened and truly civilized people.

Even when the Bhikkhu-Sangha had been newly established, and it was then a very small community consisting of only sixty monks, the Buddha sent all of its members in all directions to propagate the Dhamma. The community was then only three months old. Here, the spirit of acting for the good of the people is strongly evident. The words of the Buddha in sending out his disciples at that time reflect very well the ideal of erecting the world Noble Sangha. In the Buddha's own words (Vin.I.21):

> "Go forth, O Bhikkhus, for the good
> of the many, for the happiness of the
> many, out of compassion for the world,
> for the benefit, for the good, for the
> happiness of gods and men."

In short, the Sangha of monks or Bhikkhu-Sangha has been set up, both as the instrument and as the starting point and the stronghold, for working out the idea of establishing the universal Sangha of Dhammically civilized people. The main function of this conventional Sangha is, as mentioned earlier, to expound the Dhamma and spread it far and wide, in such a way that the common people may understand and practise it, developing themselves in their progress along the path of being Ariya (noble or Dhammically civilized) and thus joining the Noble Sangha or civilized world community. In the meantime, however, the Sangha of monks also plays a number of significant roles, some central and some interim and peripheral, such as:

-   As, especially at the beginning, the conditions in the surrounding world are not favourable to the ideal life, the Bhikkhu-Sangha serves as the suitable setting in which zealous members can energetically live their chosen way of life and leading members can actively lead others.

-   The Bhikkhu-Sangha serves as the core and leading part of the prospective Noble Sangha. By leading exemplary noble lives, the monks exercise their influence on the common people in treading the noble path towards the goal of joining the Noble Sangha.

-   The Bhikkhu-Sangha also serves as the centre for training both those who join it and the common people, to turn them into members, or make them more prepared to be members, of the Noble Sangha.

Foundations of the Sangha

In the Buddha's time, Buddhism was usually called, "This Dhamma-Vinaya" (the Doctrine and the Discipline). This means that the *Dhamma-Vinaya* is another name, actually the original name, for Buddhism. It also indicates that the Dhamma and the Vinaya are the two limbs that form Buddhism. This concept is in direct connection with the two kinds of Sangha.

The Conventional Sangha of monks depends for its existence and stability on the *Vinaya*. It is the Vinaya that gives life to the Bhikkhu-Sangha. A person is ordained a Bhikkhu or is admitted to the Sangha of monks in accordance with the rules of the Vinaya. His Bhikkhuship also ceases if he makes an incurable transgression against the Vinaya. The rules of the Vinaya govern all activities of the community of monks and all aspects of a Bhikkhu's life. Monks or Bhikkhus are graded according to concrete disciplinary rules. A Bhikkhu is classed as a *Navaka,* or a newly ordained one, if he has been admitted to the Order for not more than five years, and he is required to live in "Nissaya", or dependence, on an Ācariya or teacher, that is, he is a dependent. As soon as his years of standing in the monkhood exceed five, he becomes freed of the Dependence and is classed as a *Nissaya-Muttaka,* or an independent monk. When he completes ten years of standing in the monkhood, he becomes a *Thera* or an Elder. Now, if he is qualified, he can act as an Upajjhāya or a preceptor. Rights and privileges are vested on the Bhikkhus on equal terms according to the rules of the Vinaya.

The Noble Sangha of disciples, on the other hand, is based on the *Dhamma.* While the Vinaya governs the external life of a monk, his bodily and verbal activities and his social relations with others, his inner and spiritual side is guided by the Dhamma. Not only the monks, but all people are expected to follow the guidance of the Dhamma. In contrast to the formal admittance to membership in the conventional Sangha of monks, membership in the Noble Sangha of disciples is a matter of self-development and inner attainment. As soon as a person, whether a monk or a layman, realizes the Four Noble Truths and gains a first vision of Nibbāna, he automatically becomes a Sotāpanna and, simultaneously, a member of the Noble Sangha of disciples. His further progress on the path up to the final goal is graded solely according to the degree of his self-development and inner attainment, without the intervention of any external factors, whether age, sex, authority or even time or space. Thus, a novice twelve years of age may be an Arahant while an aged monk seventy years old may be only a worldling , not attaining even Sotāpannaship, and a wise layman may achieve Arahatship in a period of an hour while many monks may strive in vain throughout their lives to secure the same. As the Buddha says in the Dhammapada: He who, though dressed in fine apparel, exercises tranquillity, is calm, controlled, certain and chaste and has ceased to injure all other beings, he indeed is a Brāhman, a Samaṇa, a Bhikkhu. (Dh. 142)

Though the treading of the path of self-development and inner attainment is a personal task, the treader is not all alone or helpless. Besides the Great Teacher, the Buddha, who shows him the Way and equips him with the tools, the conventional Sangha of monks, as regulated by the Vinaya, provides him with *Kalyāṇamitta,* or good spiritual friends, who will counsel and encourage him along the Way, with a way of life and living conditions that are advantageous to his endeavour. In particular, those members of the Noble Sangha who are far advanced on the Path or have reached the summit, will find the Bhikkhu-Sangha the best community for them to live in, and it is these people who will best preserve the conventional Sangha of monks and will act as *Kalyāṇamitta,* or good spiritual friends, to those who are treading the Path after them.

In short, the two kinds of the Sangha are reciprocally helpful and complementary in the realization of Buddhist ideals. Without the will and effort to join or to maintain the Noble Sangha of disciples, the conventional Sangha of monks is meaningless or, at least, strays away from the ideal set up by its Founder, the Buddha. Without a concrete organization like the Bhikkhu-Sangha as the tool, the task of establishing and maintaining the Ariya-Sangha of disciples would be very difficult, if not an impossibility.

The Real Mission of the Sangha

There is no doubt that peace and freedom are the supreme goals of Buddhism. Both of them are synonyms of Nibbāna or Nirvāna. Peace can be realized, and freedom can be achieved, if the Sangha of monks exerts itself unfalteringly to maintain and universalize the Noble Sangha of disciples.

Freedom is threefold or can be distinguished at three levels. First, people should enjoy the basic freedom of life in absence of the fundamental insecurities and dangers that threaten their existence, such as poverty, diseases and calamities like drought and famine. Without the minimum of this basic freedom, no one can proceed to enjoy any other more sublime freedom. At the second level is social freedom, in absence of human oppression and exploitation. Included here are tolerance, friendliness and benevolence. With the lack of this freedom, not to speak of the final freedom, even the basic freedom will never be realized or, if the latter has been prevailing, it will surely be lost. The third and last is the final freedom of man's inner life, that is, freedom from mental suffering and from the greed, hatred and delusion that corrupt the mind and cause people to commit all kinds of evils. With the achievement of this level of freedom, real happiness can be attained to and social freedom can be assured. It is also the firm foundation on which to work out any plan or programme to overcome the basic insecurities and dangers of life, as otherwise people with corrupted mind will ever increase those dangers and insecurities.

In another classification, freedom is said to be fourfold. There, the final inner or individual freedom is divided into the two levels of emotional freedom, or freedom of the heart, and intellectual freedom, or freedom of wisdom through true knowledge. The four levels of freedom are thus distinguished as basic physical freedom, social freedom, emotional freedom and intellectual freedom.

By teaching and encouraging people to realize the three graded goals and the three phases of good as enunciated by the Buddha, the Sangha of monks works both directly and indirectly to achieve the threefold freedom.

The three graded goals are:

1. Benefits for the present or temporal welfare, called in Pali *Diṭṭhadhammikattha,* represented by wealth, sufficiency of food and other necessities of life, health and other aspects of physical well-being, which can be ascertained by hard work, diligence,

good management, cooperation, economical living and non-negligence in any way.

2. Benefits for the future, or spiritual welfare, called in Pali *Samparāyikattha,* as ensured by confidence in and devotion to the ways of the good, morality, benevolence, wisdom and other virtues.

3. The supreme benefit or the highest good, called in Pali *Paramattha,* consisting in having a mind that is clean and clear, happy and secure, undefiled by greed, hatred and delusion, and unshaken by worldly vicissitudes, that is to say, the final freedom of Nibbāna.

The three phases of good are:

1. The good of one's own or one's own welfare, *Attattha,* which points to the above three graded goals as realized by oneself.

2. The good of others or others' welfare, *Parattha,* referring to the same set of three

graded goals which one should guide or help others to attain.

3. The common good or welfare both of oneself and others, *Ubhayattha,* identified with the same set of three graded goals as far as they should be shared by all concerned, ranging from public utilities and favourable environment to peace and happiness of the mind.

The first two graded goals secure for all people freedom from the basic miseries and insecurities of life and freedom from social abuses such as aggression, crime, oppression and exploitation. People who are endowed with these two grades of freedom are in a good position or are better prepared to aspire to the highest good and to enjoy the final freedom. By conducting oneself towards the realization of the final freedom, one comes to join the Noble Sangha of disciples. Those who enjoy the final freedom will ever fortify and strengthen the first two grades of freedom, as the final freedom is a guarantee of the maintenance of the latter. Moreover, the practices along the line of realizing the three phases of good even furthermore reinforce the establishment of the three grades of freedom.

All in all, it is the mission of the Sangha of monks to work for the prevailing of the three graded goals and the three phases of good, for the realization of the three levels of freedom and thus, ideally, for the establishment and perpetuation of the Noble Sangha of disciples.

Not unlike freedom, peace should be classified. Peace is of two kinds, one is external and the other, internal. External peace is usually social. It is freedom from strife, dissension, quarrelling, commotion, violence, disorder and, on the largest scale, war. Internal peace is the inner peace of mind or spiritual peace. It is a state of freedom from fear, anxiety, annoyance, distraction, obsession and, on the minutest scale, from all traces of mental suffering and defilement. It is obvious that without freedom, there can be no peace. Once freedom is secured, peace is attained to.

As with freedom, the Sangha has much to do with both external and internal peace. The Sangha of monks paves the way through external peace to the inner peace of the final freedom and, once the Noble Sangha is established with this inner peace, a firm foundation has been laid on which the external social peace will rest securely and lastingly.

Evolution of the Monastic Sangha

The importance of the conventional Sangha of monks as the principal agent for expanding and perpetuating the Noble Sangha of disciples has been realized throughout the long history of Buddhism. Thus, a small Sangha of monks was dispatched to foreign lands or distant places to spread Buddhism. Often, only one monk or a group of two or three monks were sent out to do this task and the monk or the group had to depend on local men to believe and ordain before a local Sangha of monks could be established.

In the early periods, especially at the beginning of the career of the Buddha, the members of the Sangha of monks were also *Ariya,* or members of the Noble Sangha. Their mission, therefore, turned only outward to increase the membership in the Noble Sangha and to receive those who were willing and prepared into the monastic Sangha. As time went on and the monastic Sangha became greatly enlarged, the number of members of the monastic Sangha who were not yet entitled to the membership in the Noble Sangha increased. The monastic Sangha then functioned more and more as the centre for training the unenlightened members, and the energy of the leaders in the monastic Sangha had to be divided between the inside and the outside of the monasteries, sometimes too much on the inside, to the neglect of the mission for the benefit of the outside. However, generally speaking, once a monastic Sangha has been established in a land, Buddhism is established there.

The different monastic Sanghas in different lands and countries lived and worked in different surroundings and among peoples of different cultures. With the passing of time, throughout the centuries, they developed some new roles and traditions of their own which were local. Some of these roles and traditions developed even at the expense of the original fundamental function of perpetuating the Noble Sangha of disciples. In spite of all local differences, however, the Vinaya keeps the various local monastic Sanghas, although geographically far apart, not too dissimilar to one another.

It is impossible to treat here of all the monastic Sanghas in so many different countries. As the Thai Sangha of today is said to be the largest monastic community in the world, it will be dealt with here as an example.

The Monastic Tradition in Thailand

The monastic tradition in Thailand can be traced back to the time of King Asoka when, around B.E. 234 (310 B.C.), nine missions of monks were sent out as Dhamma messengers to propagate the Dhamma in different countries. One of the missions, headed by the Elders Soṇa and Uttara, came to Suvaṇṇabhūmi which covered some parts of what we now call Thailand, and succeeded in establishing Buddhism there. We do not know much about the Buddhist situations and developments later than that time until the foundation of the present lineage of the *Thai monastic Sangha* in the Sukhothai period, around B.E. 1820 (1277 C.E.). We learn that at the time when the present form of monastic Sangha of the Laṅkāvaṁsa tradition was established in Sukhothai, there prevailed monks of some older local traditions. Before long, the monks of the older traditions became absorbed into the newly established Sangha.

The present tradition of Thai monastic Sangha was established under the full support of the King who himself invited the head monk from afar to found it and since then, throughout the different periods of over 700 years, it has enjoyed the status of the national Sangha under royal patronage and state protection. At present, the large Thai monastic community consists of about 400,000 monks and novices who are accommodated in more than 30,000 monasteries all over the country. In comparison with the whole Thai population of 48 million, of which about 93.4 percent are Buddhist, it makes Thailand deserve the name of the "Land of the Yellow Robe". The fact that such a large monastic community fares well under the support of a Buddhist population of that size shows clearly how devout and generous the Thai Buddhists are.

Right from the beginning, the Thai monastic Sangha has been divided into two sections, *town-monks* and *forest-monks.* The division is only a matter of specialization and there is a good relationship between the two, including the transfer of residents. Forest monks preserve the tradition of meditation, while town-monks specialize in study and engage in religio-cultural activities. In comparison with town monasteries, the number of forest monasteries is small.

The over 30,000 monasteries are also classified into two categories of royal monasteries and private or community ones. Royal monasteries are those erected by the King or having obtained his recognition. They are usually large and contain imposing edifices. Community monasteries are mostly smaller and simple. Only about 200 monasteries are royal and most of them are in the capital, while the majority are private or community ones scattered in the villages throughout the country.

The kings of Ayudhya, beginning 600 years ago, were much influenced by Brahminism and Brahmin advisers were consulted in cultural and administrative affairs. Consequently, Brahminical rites and ceremonies have continued in state activities side by side with the Buddhist ones. This has sometimes led to the mingling of the two. At the village level, the populace have been more or less attached to animistic beliefs and practices. Through the monks' association with these villagers, some animistic elements have crept into Buddhism. With the integration of animistic and Brahminical elements into Buddhism in the process of assimilation, there has developed a form of popular Buddhism, in which rites and ceremonies are predominant and superstitious beliefs and practices are prevalent.

Town and village monasteries have been, for Thais of all classes, centres of education, both religious and secular. There, basic subjects like reading, writing and arithmetic were taught to boys. The Thais have also developed a custom of *temporary ordination*. Every young man is expected to stay for a period of about three months (usually in the Vassa or the rainy season) in a monastery as a monk. Here it is education for socializing male members of the society, as they are expected to join the monkhood to undergo monastic and cultural training before running families and assuming other civic responsibilities, including civil and military services, as learned ex-monks. This custom has, however, been on the decline during the last half of the century.

Since the introduction of the modern Western system of education to the country about a century ago, Thailand has been experiencing the problem of inequality of opportunity in education, as large numbers of poor and underprivileged youngsters in the upcountry villages cannot get access to public and higher education. The monasteries have done much to help ease the situation as the monkhood has been the channel of education for these sons of the peasants and villagers from distant areas. Thus, the monastic systems of education in present-day Thailand, whether the traditional system of Pali and Dhamma studies, or the two Buddhist universities in Bangkok, together with their affiliated colleges in the provinces, not only provide monastic learning for monks and novices, but also serve the educational needs of the Thai society as a whole.

Monasteries have been seats of Thai culture and Buddhism has been a foundation of the Thai culture. Arts and architecture have been developed and preserved in the monasteries. A large number of Thai words, especially almost all technical terms, are derived from Pali and Sanskrit. Thai literature has been based to a large extent on Buddhist literature. In fact, most of the Thai literary works in the past were Buddhist in nature and were written by monks in the monasteries. Besides, the monasteries have been centres of social activities, where people assemble in large gatherings, both on religious and on civic occasions, including temple fairs.

Although, since the arising of the *Dhammayut* group (also called *Dhammayuttikā*) about one and a half centuries ago, the Thai monastic Sangha has been divided into two denominations or suborders of the *Mahānikāya* and the *Dhammayut,* the whole monastic community is still unified under one and the same governing body, called the Council of Elders, or the Sangha Supreme Council, presided over by the Supreme Patriarch. The State has enacted laws forming a Constitution under which the monastic Sangha governs itself. According to the present act of B.E. 2505 (1962 C.E.), the Sangha administration is based on the process of centralisation. The Supreme Patriarch, who is appointed by the King, has absolute power to govern the whole monastic community and to direct all ecclesiastical affairs. Under him is the Sangha Supreme Council, which serves him as the Consultative Council. Under this highest governing body, at the local administrative level, 73 ecclesiastical provincial governors are responsible for provincial affairs of the Sangha, each in his respective province.

The Sangha, the State and the Ideal World Community

In carrying out its mission, the main concern of the monastic Sangha is surely the good and happiness of the people. However, throughout its history, all evidence shows that the Bhikkhu-Sangha has been in relationship with another central institution of the society, that is, the state, as represented by the king or the ruler. In the Buddha's time, King Bimbisāra and King Pasenadi were in close personal relationship with the Buddha and were patrons of the Bhikkhu-Sangha. In Thai history, the monastic Sangha, by tradition, have been patronized by all the kings.

There are at least two reasons that account for this relationship. First, the people are subjects of the state. Their destinies, their suffering and happiness are to a large extent subject to the conditions of the state and to the acts of the king or ruler. For any organization to deal with the people as a whole or to work for their benefit, it is impossible to avoid some contact with the state or with the ruler. Because of this, if possible, a good relationship should be maintained with the state, so that the Sangha will find no difficulty in working for the welfare of the people.

Secondly, the goal of a good government is similar to that of the Sangha, that is, the achievement of the good and happiness for the people. Then, if the government or the ruler is a good one, the cooperation between the Sangha and the ruler or the government will render the mission more effective. The government or the ruler can even be a medium through which the monastic Sangha carries out its mission for the good of the people. At least, a good government or ruler can provide the people with conditions and circumstances that are favourable to the practice of the Dhamma.

Accordingly, the duties of the monastic Sangha in connection with the state or ruler are twofold. First, it should counsel him so that he is a good ruler or that a good government is secured. Secondly, it should act in such a righteous way that there will be good cooperation with the ruler or the government in operating for the benefit of the people, or at least that the way will be open for the Sangha to achieve that goal. On the whole, the point is that the secular part of the work for the good of the people should be played by one who should account for it, that is, the ruler or government. If he does not do so, it is also an obligation of the monastic Sangha to see to it that he does, that is, to try to induce him to be a good ruler. The real monastic part of the work under the charge of the Sangha is the more sublime inner life of man.

Although the monastic Sangha has developed new roles, whether central or peripheral, whether temporary or lasting, through the different circumstances of space and time, its real and fundamental mission remains the same all throughout the ages, that is, to perpetuate the Noble Sangha of disciples. In the future, the monastic Sangha, because of the factors of space and time, may have to change some existing roles and play some more different ones, but as long as it keeps to the real mission, the spirit of the Sangha is well preserved. The reason is that the conventional Sangha of monks has been entrusted by the Buddha the task of leading all people in creating the ideal world community of noble disciples or truly civilized people.

Let us hope that all the members of the Sangha of monks will exert themselves and cooperate with one another in working out the ideal of producing more and more members of the Noble Sangha of disciples, and that Sangha of disciples will grow ever more for the freedom, peace and happiness of all mankind.

INDEX

About the author

Born on Thursday, 12 January, 1939 (B.E. 2481),
Ordained as a novice on 10 May 1951 (2494),
Received higher ordination under the sponsorship of *King Bhumibol Adulyadej* on the 24th of July 1961 (2504) at *Wat Phra Kaew* - the "Temple of the Emerald Buddha" with the Supreme Patriarch as preceptor.

EDUCATION:

Passed Pali IX, the highest level of Pāli studies (while still a novice), 1961 (2504),
Bachelor Degree in Buddhist Studies (1st-class honors),1962(2505),
Higher Certificate in Education 1963 (2506),
Honorary Doctorate in Buddhist Studies, Mahachulalongkorn Buddhist University,1982 (2525),
Honorary Doctorate in Philosophy, Thammasat University,1986 (2529),
Honorary Doctorate in Education, Silapakorn University,1987 (2530),
Honorary Doctorate in Education, Kasetsart University,1987 (2530),
Honorary Doctorate in Linguistics, Chulalongkorn University,1988 (2531),
Honorary Doctorate in Linguistics, Mahidol University, 1989 (2532),
Honorary Doctorate in Education, Srinakarinvirot University, 1990 (2533).

TITLES:

1969 (2512), received the royal title "Phra Srivisuddhimoli";
1973 (2516), received the higher royal title "Phra Rajavaramuni";
1987 (2530), received the higher royal title "Phra Debvedi".

DUTIES AND WORK:

1962 (2505) - 1963 (2506), served as full-time instructor at the Pāli Pre-university school, Mahachulalongkorn Buddhist University;

1964 (2507) - 1974 (2517), received the position of Assistant to the Secretary-General, and later became Deputy Secretary-General of Mahachula.

From 1967 to 1968 (2510-11), he went to Laos, Sri Lanka, Malaysia, Singapore, Hong Kong, Taiwan, Korea and Japan; and in 1972 (2515) he was asked to lecture at the University of Pennsylvania, in 1976 (2519) Swarthmore College, and in 1981 (2524) Harvard University.

LITERARY WORKS:

Among his literary works are:

Dictionary of Buddhism (Bangkok: Mahachula Buddhist University, 1972-5 /2515-18),

Buddhadharma (Bangkok: Dharmasatharn, Chulalongkorn University, 1982/2525),

Thai Buddhism in the Buddhist World (Bangkok: Mahachula Buddhist University, 1987/2530),

Social Dimension of Buddhism in Contemporary Thailand (Bangkok: Thaikhadi Research Institute, Thammasat University, 1983/2526),

Freedom: Individual and Social (Bangkok: Buddhadhamma Foundation, Printed for free distribution , 1987/2530).

Sammāsati. Tr. by Dhamma-Vijaya. (Bangkok: Buddhadhamma Foundation, Printed for free distribution, 1990/2533).

Helping Yourself to Help Others (Bangkok: Buddhadhamma Foundation, Printed for free distribution, 1990/2533).